The Body of Christ and Israel

God's Family in Heaven and on Earth

Jeffery Drake, Jr.

TRUST HOUSE PUBLISHERS

Taos, New Mexico

The Body of Christ and Israel: God's Family in Heaven and on Earth

All Scriptures are quoted from the King James Version (KJV).

Published by:
Trust House Publishers
P.O. Box 3181
Taos, NM 87571
www.TrustHousePublishers.com

ISBN: 978-1-961110-39-7

Ordering Information:
Quantity sales. Special discounts are available on quantity purchases by churches, associations, and others. For details, contact the publisher at the address above or by phone at 1-844-321-4202.

Printed in the United States of America

1 2 3 4 5 6 7 8 9

Contents

Introduction

In Ephesians 3:9, the Bible speaks about making all men see what is the fellowship of the mystery, which from the beginning of the world hath been hid in God, who created all things by Jesus Christ. This is exactly the purpose of this book. Understanding the mystery of Christ, which God gave to the apostle Paul to reveal to us, is vitally important to understanding the Bible. This book is not written to please any particular denomination. This book is written to reveal the mystery that God kept secret until He revealed it to Paul (Ephesians 3:1-12). Every word in this book is written based on the uncompromising belief that the King James Bible is perfect and without error. When reading this book, it would be best to have a KJB next to you, so you can check scripture references as needed. The whole Bible is given to us to study and increase in the knowledge of God. This book will teach you to do what 2 Timothy 2:15 commands. Which is to be workmen that rightly divide the word of truth.

(Colossians 4:2-4) 2 Continue in prayer, and watch in the same with thanksgiving; 3 Withal praying also for us, that God would open unto us a door of utterance, to speak the mystery of Christ, for which I am also in bonds: 4 That I may make it manifest, as I ought to speak.

1

The Nation Israel

In Genesis chapter 12, God chose Abraham as His vessel through whom He would bring forth His favored nation, which is Israel. Through this chosen nation, eventually all the earth would be blessed. They were to be a special nation, set apart to take the knowledge of the true God to all the earth. Abraham had a son Isaac and Isaac had a son named Jacob. Jacob eventually had twelve sons and out from them came forth the twelve tribes that formed the nation, Israel (Acts 7:8). God made the covenants of circumcision and the law with this nation. These covenants were to set Israel apart from all other nations. The law was dispensed to Israel through God's chosen spokesman to that nation, which was the man, Moses. The covenant of the law between God and Israel included the ten commandments, the priesthood, the sacrificial system, and many other statutes that added up to more than six hundred laws. This is what the New Testament refers to as the first covenant (Hebrews 8:7).

The promises made to Israel were conditional. By conditional I mean the blessings promised to Israel in the first covenant (the law of Moses) would be received only if they by faith kept and performed the statutes of the covenant. They had to have faith plus the required works to receive the blessings. If they failed to keep God's statutes according to the covenant, they would receive curses rather than blessings. These things are very clearly laid out in Deuteronomy 30:15-20 and Leviticus chapter 26. God promised Israel that He would put them in a land that would produce abundantly and provide for the nation. Joshua led them into the promised land and the land was divided among the twelve tribes to form the nation, Israel. Israel had no king but rather God gave them judges about the space of 450 years, until Samuel the prophet. Instead of being God's unique holy nation they desired to be like the other nations and wanted to have a king. This was an act of disobedience. The LORD gave them Saul to be their king for 40 years. Saul was disobedient to God, and after He removed Saul, He raised up David to be their king. The Bible says in Acts 13:22, "I have found David the son of Jesse, a man after mine own heart, which shall fulfil all my will." The LORD told David (Psalm 132:11) that "of the fruit of thy body will I sit upon thy throne for evermore." This was fulfilled when Mary, who was of the lineage of David, conceived miraculously as a virgin, by the work of the Holy Ghost, and gave birth to Jesus. God was manifest in the flesh (1 Timothy 3:16) and the ministry of John the Baptist was to prepare Israel to receive their King and His kingdom on earth.

The books Matthew, Mark, Luke, and John record the ministry of Jesus, the Son of God, according to what was prophesied about Him in the Old Testament (Luke 24:44). Our Lord's ministry at this time was to only the nation Israel and not the Gentiles (Matthew 10:5,6) (Matthew 15:24) (John 4:22) (Romans 15:8). Gentiles simply means "nations." In the Bible a Gentile is anyone that is not a Jew (Romans 2:9). It is particularly important that we understand that in these four books God is dealing with Israel, which is under the Old Testament law of Moses (Matthew 8:4). The doctrine in these books is not aimed at us today in God's present dispensation of grace (Ephesians 3:1,2). In these books we learn history about Israel concerning the promised Christ (Psalm 132:11), who came to Israel preaching the gospel of the kingdom (Matthew 4:23). Satan and his devils were in the land at that time. They were there to disrupt Christ's ministry and were trying to prevent the establishment of God's kingdom on earth. When Christ was on the cross Satan thought he was winning the battle. However, God in His infinite wisdom defeated sin, death, and the devil through

Christ's death, burial, and resurrection (1 Corinthians 2:6-8) (1 Corinthians 15:55-57) (Hebrews 2:14).

In Matthew, Mark, Luke, and John, Christ is dividing the nation between believers in Him and unbelievers (Luke 12:51) (John 7:43). The Lord is calling out a believing remnant of Jews, and after that is accomplished, His focus turns to the cross. Also, it is important to understand some things about the parables spoken by Jesus in these books. Parables are similar to riddles, in that unless we know key information, we cannot clearly understand the meaning. A great example is in Luke 8:4-15. The Lord tells a large audience the parable of the Sower, and the people do not clearly understand the meaning. In verse 9, the true believers ask Him what the parable means. In verse 10, the Lord tells the believers that He is speaking in parables so that the unbelievers would not understand the meaning of what He said. He will go on in verses 11-15 to explain in clear understandable language the meaning of the parable, but only to the believers. So, when reading these books do not get frustrated if you do not completely comprehend the meaning of the parables. The purpose of the parables is to make information more difficult to understand, not easier. Sometimes the Lord will go on and explain the meaning, but not always. When you hear a preacher suggesting they know the meaning of a parable that Christ does not expound upon, beware that the preacher may not understand the meaning as well as they think they do. Jesus spoke in parables to purposely communicate truth that people could not understand (Matthew 13:13-15). The real believers would come to him seeking the meaning of the parable. This was one way He was separating believers from unbelievers. The parables communicate truth about God's kingdom with Israel, and they are meant to be difficult to understand.

The gospel message being declared in Matthew, Mark, Luke, and John, is called the gospel of the kingdom (Matthew 4:23) (Matthew 9:35). Signs and miracles accompany this message. This gospel (good news) is about the promised "Christ" (Psalm 132:11) and His everlasting kingdom on earth (Daniel 4:3) (Daniel 7:27) (Luke 1:33). The signs and miracles that the Lord and His apostles were performing were prophesied in the Old Testament (Psalm 146:8) (Daniel 4:3) (Zechariah 13:2). If the leaders in Israel had been reading and believing the scriptures, they should have been able to identify Jesus as the Christ (the Son of God) and believed that the kingdom was truly at hand. However, the majority of the nation lacked faith and did not believe the gospel of the kingdom. The Lord's ministry in these books divided the nation between unbelievers and a remnant of true believers (Luke 12:51).

The gospel of the kingdom did not include Christ's death on the cross for the redemption of the sins of mankind, or His victorious resurrection. This is a biblical fact that is very important to understand, because the gospel that Christ gave to the apostle Paul, which is the gospel by which we are saved today is "how that Christ died for our sins, and was buried, and that he rose again the third day" (1 Corinthians 15:1-4). In Luke 9:6 the Bible says, the twelve apostles were preaching the gospel everywhere, then in Luke 18:31-34, we are told that the apostles understood "NOTHING" about Christ's death and resurrection. In John 20:3-9, we see that shortly after the Lord's resurrection, Peter and John still did not understand the resurrection. It is extremely important to understand that the gospel of the kingdom being preached in Matthew, Mark, Luke, and John, is not the same message as the gospel that Christ later revealed to the apostle Paul (Galatians 1:11,12). The gospel of grace (Acts 20:24)) given to Paul, is the gospel we trust today, to receive eternal life (Romans 1:16) (1 Corinthians 15:14). The gospel of the kingdom was about believing Jesus is Christ (the Son of God and King) and being water baptized in His name (Mark 16:16). In John 3:16, when it speaks about believing in the only begotten Son of God, verse 18 makes it clear, that it is faith in His name, not His death, burial, and resurrection. John 20:31, also makes this fact abundantly clear.

We will address something that most of Christendom gets wrong. This is Matthew chapters 5-7. These chapters are commonly referred to as "the sermon on the mount." In these chapters Christ is speaking to Israel with the authority of a king (Matthew 7:29). He communicates the statutes concerning the kingdom that was at hand. This message gives us information about living in a moral and godly way, however this message is to Israel and for Israel, who were at that time under the law of Moses. Today we are not under the law, but under grace (Romans 6:14). While there is a lesson to learn about morality, the doctrine in these chapters is not directed at us in God's current dispensation of grace to Gentiles (Ephesians 3:1,2). The books of Matthew, Mark, Luke, and John were written about the nation Israel when that nation was still operating under the old covenant law of Moses. This included the ten commandments, the priesthood, the system of animal sacrifice, feast days, and many more things which the Bible calls "the Jews religion" (Galatians 1:14). There are many verses that show us these four books are not written under God's current dispensation of grace, but rather under the law of Moses. This is a short list of those verses (Matthew 5:23,24) (Matthew 8:4) (Luke 10:25-28) (Luke 23:56). One more very clear passage that shows us the doctrine in these four books is for Israel under the law and not for us under grace, is Matthew 6:14,15. These verses clearly teach that to be forgiven sins, they must forgive others. Today under God's current dispensation of grace to Gentiles (Ephesians 3:1,2), we are to be forgiving people, because we that are saved have already been forgiven by God (Ephesians 4:32). Today the moment we believe the gospel of our salvation (1 Corinthians 15:1-4), which is "that Christ shed His blood and died on the cross for our sins, and that He was buried, and that He rose again the third day," we receive forgiveness of sins and the gift of eternal life (Romans 1:16) (Romans 6:23) (Ephesians 1:7) (Ephesians 1:13) (Ephesians 2:8,9). The gospel of our salvation today was not yet revealed in Matthew, Mark, Luke, or John.

After the Lord's resurrection and before He ascends to heaven, He gives instructions to the apostles. In Matthew 28:18-20, we see the Lord's instructions are to go and teach all nations, baptizing them in the name of the Father, Son, and of the Holy Ghost. This message is commonly called "the great commission." However, very few compare these verses with other verses which give us more details about this "great commission." We must let the scripture be the final authority and not the tradition of men.

When we read Luke 24:27, which is another account of these instructions. We see that this message is not aimed at the "nations" themselves, but rather "among" all nations. Next, when we look at John 20:21, the resurrected Lord tells the apostles, "as my Father hath sent me, even so send I you." Then when we read Matthew 15:24, we see that the Father sent Christ to the Jews only. In Acts 10:28, after Peter is forced by the Spirit of God, to preach to the Gentiles, the first thing he says to the Gentiles is that "it is an unlawful thing for a man that is a Jew to keep company, or come unto one of another nation." Keep in mind this is Acts chapter 10, which is after the Lord gave the "great commission." After preaching to Gentiles Peter returns to the Jews in Jerusalem, and in Acts 11:1-3, these Jews which are under the "great commission" were upset with Peter for going to Gentiles. Hang in there as we are showing from the Bible that the "great commission" in Matthew 28:18-20, is for Jews only. Some might run to Acts 2:39, where Peter says to Israel, "the promise is unto you, and your children, and to all that are afar off." When we cross reference this with Daniel 9:7, we see that "to all that are afar off," is speaking of Jews which are scattered among the nations. The last point we will make to show the "great commission" is to Jews only, is in the book of Acts as well. In Acts 8:4, we see that the disciples which were scattered by Saul's persecution, "went everywhere preaching the word." Then when we come to Acts 11:19, we see that these scattered disciples were preaching the word to "JEWS" only. It is very important to understand the instructions given in Matthew 28:18-20, is focused on Jews in Israel and Jews which were scattered among the nations. These instructions are not to and about you and me, who are operating in the present dispensation of God's grace to Gentiles. Now, after looking at the testimony of scripture, when we read Mark 16:15, "Go ye into all the world and preach the gospel to every creature," and Matthew 28:19, "Go ye therefore, and teach all nations," as Acts 11:19 tells us, this is speaking about every Jew among all nations. In Acts 2:5, the same apostles to whom were given the "great commission" were preaching to Jews, out of every nation under heaven. Today we should be preaching the gospel of our salvation to every person under heaven, but our message is not water baptism, but rather Christ's shed blood and death for our sins, and His burial, and resurrection, as the power of God unto salvation to every one that believeth (1 Corinthians 1:17,18) (Romans 1:16).

The main focus of the book of Acts is the nation Israel and their rejection of the gospel of the kingdom in chapters 1-12, and their rejection of the gospel of the grace of God in chapters 13-28. In Acts 2:16-21, Peter makes it very clear that what is beginning to take place at that time is the "last days" prophesied by the prophet Joel. These last days, according to Acts 2:16-21, would lead to the day of the Lord, which will be a time of great tribulation and wrath upon this evil world. In Acts chapters 1-7, we see the twelve apostles going to Israel with the gospel of the kingdom. By that time this gospel message includes Christ's victorious resurrection. Only a remnant of the nation believed this message and receive the required water baptism. The majority of the nation, including the religious leaders, reject this message. In Acts chapter 7, Stephen is addressing leaders in Israel, and he walks them through their history of rejecting God. Instead of repenting and believing that Jesus is Christ (the Son of God), they reject the truth and stone Stephen to death. In Acts 7:55, just before they kill him, Stephen looks up to heaven and tells them he sees Jesus standing. Isaiah 3:13 says, "The LORD standeth up to plead, and standeth up to judge the people." Some teach that the reason Jesus is standing is because He was ready to pour out His wrath and judgment on this world. This is not correct because according to Daniel Chapter 11:21-23, the final seven-year period of judgment before Christ returns as the King, cannot begin until the antichrist (man of sin) has been revealed and risen to power. At the stoning of Stephen, the antichrist was not yet on the scene. Remember, Isaiah 3:13 says, "The Lord standeth up to plead, and standeth to judge the people." The reason Stephen saw the Lord standing is because in the first seven chapters of Acts, He is "pleading" with Israel. After they kill Stephen, the Lord sits back down at the Father's right hand and the time of pleading with the nation is over. The next time the Lord stands concerning Israel, it will be time for judgment and wrath (Revelation 19:11- 16).

The focus of the book of Acts from beginning to end is the nation, Israel. This book can be described as a transitional book. After the religious leaders and elders in Jerusalem reject the gospel of the kingdom (Acts 4:17) (Acts 5:40) (Acts 7:57), God then moves His focus outside of Jerusalem. This begins in Acts chapter 8. In Acts chapter 9, the Lord makes an unforetold "mystery" appearance to His enemy at the time, Saul of Tarsus. In the Bible from Genesis chapter 12 until we get to Acts chapter 9, God was focusing on and working through the nation Israel. The Gentiles at this time had no hope (Ephesians 2:11,12). Gentiles could get circumcised and proselytize into the nation Israel. In Acts 9:15, God calls Saul (who is Paul) His chosen vessel to go to the Gentiles. This special ministry given to Paul was not foretold in the Old Testament. Beginning in Acts chapter 13, we read that God sends the apostle Paul to the Gentile world with the gospel of the grace of God (Acts 20:24). We read in Acts 13:39 that this new message is justification by faith, without the works of the law. We also see that this new message is salvation by faith, without water baptism (Acts 16:31). However, to get a deep understanding of the gospel of the grace of God, we must study Paul's epistles of Romans through Philemon. The focus of the book of Acts is not doctrine, but rather the history of Israel rejecting the gospel of the kingdom and then rejecting the gospel of the grace of God. The book of Acts also records the transition from God dealing with primarily Jews, then after Acts 28:28, He is dealing with primarily Gentiles. Much more could be said about the book of Acts but that is not the focus of this book.

2

The Apostle Paul

After the transitional book of Acts, comes the apostle Paul's thirteen books, Romans through Philemon. When Paul first appears in the Bible he is called Saul, which is his Hebrew name. At the end of Acts chapter 7, Saul is supervising the murder of Stephen. In the beginning of Acts chapter 8, we learn that Saul is persecuting the church, which is Israel's believing remnant. At this time Saul was the enemy of Jesus Christ, and he was bent on punishing anyone that believed Jesus is the Son of God. When we get to Acts chapter 9, we see that Saul gets permission from Israel's high priest to leave Jerusalem and hunt down believers and bring them to Jerusalem to be punished. On his journey, as he neared the city of Damascus, something amazing takes place. The Lord Jesus, in an unforetold return, appears unto his enemy, Saul of Tarsus. In Acts 9:15, we learn that Christ is sending Saul as His chosen vessel to the Gentiles. From Genesis chapter 12, with the calling of Abraham until Acts 9:15, God's focus has been the nation of Israel. The Lord Jesus shows amazing grace by appearing to His enemy, the unbeliever Saul, and making him a preacher, and an apostle, and a teacher of the Gentiles (2 Timothy 1:11). This appearing of the Lord, and the ministry He gives to Saul, is the very beginning of an unforetold mystery, which Ephesians 3:1-3 calls the dispensation of the grace of God, to the Gentiles.

We see in Acts 9:15, that Paul is God's chosen vessel to go to the Gentiles. However, his ministry begins as a fellow minister with the other apostles to Israel (Acts 9:27,28) (Acts 26:20). It is in Acts chapter 13 that God begins ushering in His dispensation of grace to the Gentiles. In Acts 13:2, the Holy Ghost "separates" Saul and Barnabas for this purpose. In Romans 1:1, Paul says he is "separated" unto the gospel of God, and Acts chapter 13 is when this happened. In Acts 13:9, is the first time we see Saul called "Paul." After this verse he is always called Paul, and the Bible never calls him Saul again, except when Paul retells what took place in Acts chapter 9. This marks the beginning of Paul's ministry concerning the gospel of the grace of God (Acts 20:24) to the heathen world, which includes Gentiles and Jews that had not yet believed in Jesus Christ. Starting in Acts 13:4, Paul is sent on his first apostolic journey from the church at Antioch. In Acts 14:26-28, Paul returns from his journey to the church at Antioch. This apostolic journey which began in Acts chapter 13, is when the gospel of our salvation today is first preached to the Gentiles. We know this because when Paul returns to the church at Antioch, he tells them that God has opened the door of faith unto the Gentiles (Acts 14:27). In Acts 15:23, it speaks about believing Gentiles at Antioch, however these are Gentiles that believed after Paul's return to Antioch, when he revealed that the door of faith was now opened to the Gentiles. If Paul was already going to Gentiles before he departed from Antioch in Acts 13:4, then he would have had no need to tell them upon his return that the door of faith was opened to the Gentiles. It was when Paul returned to Antioch and (Acts 14:28) abode there a long time, that the gospel went to Gentiles at Antioch. When Paul gets saved in Acts chapter 9, God is still focusing on calling out a remnant of believing Jews. In Acts 13:2, Paul is "separated" from Israel's believing remnant, and this is when God begins forming the "church" which is the body of Christ.

In the first twelve chapters of the book of Acts, God is working through His twelve apostles. They are preaching the gospel of the Kingdom, which now includes the Lord's resurrection. In Acts 2:16-21, Peter declares to Israel, that the last days which would lead to the day of the Lord's wrath and His return to earth to set up His kingdom, had begun. In Acts chapter 13, God paused His prophetic fulfillment concerning Israel, and He began to usher in and reveal a mystery dispensation that had been kept secret since the world began. This new operation of God was first revealed to Paul, and Paul explains it to us in his epistles (Romans 16:25,26) (Ephesians 3:1-9) (Colossians 1:25,26). From Acts chapter 13 to the end of that book the focus is Paul's ministry to Jews and Gentiles. His ministry concerns what Paul calls in Acts 20:24, the gospel of the grace of God, which concerns God's will for the heavens. God's kingdom includes the heavens and the earth (1 Chronicles 29:11). We do not get the details of this gospel in the book of Acts. The main focus of the book of Acts is Israel's fall (Romans 11:12). In Acts chapters 1-12, Israel as a majority reject the gospel of the kingdom, which was preached by Peter, James, and John. In Acts chapters 13-28, most of the Jews that Paul preached to reject the gospel of the grace of God. During the book of Acts, Paul goes to the Jew first, and also to the Gentile (Romans 1:16). At the close of the book of Acts in Acts 28:28, Paul tells the Jews that the salvation of God is sent to the Gentiles. After the close of the time period covered by the book of Acts, the gospel of the grace of God is still available to the Jews, however Paul's main focus turns from the Jews unto the Gentiles. In order to learn about God's dispensation of grace to the Gentiles, which is what God is doing today, we must study Romans through Philemon to get the details. When the King James Bible uses the word "dispensation," it means a dispensing or dealing out of information or instructions from God to mankind, which lets us know what God is doing and how He is operating. This word is used four times in the Bible, and all four occurrences are in Paul's epistles. In Ephesians 3:1-2, the Bible tells us that the dispensation of grace was given to Paul to give to us Gentiles. In Romans 6:14, Paul tells us we are not under the law, but under grace. From that statement we know that the law of Moses was a dispensation of God. God dispensed His law to Moses to give to the nation Israel. God dispensed His grace to the apostle Paul to give to the Gentiles. Paul's apostleship is unique and distinctly different and separate from James, Peter, John, and the rest of Israel's apostles. The first verse in the Bible tells us that God created the heaven and the earth. God has a purpose for heaven, and He has a purpose for the earth. He will work through Israel to fulfill His eternal purpose for the earth, and He will work through us, the body of Christ, to fulfill His eternal purpose for the heavens. James, Peter, and John are ministers of God's prophetic program, which is spoken of by all the Old Testament prophets. Paul is a minister of God's mystery program, which was kept secret since the world began, until God revealed it to the apostle Paul.

It is vitally important that we pay very close attention to what the Bible tells us about the apostle Paul and his unique ministry. The Bible is very clear that Paul is God's messenger to the Gentiles in this present dispensation of grace. Romans 11:13, tells us that Paul is the apostle of the Gentiles. Ephesians 3:1, tells us Paul is the prisoner of Jesus Christ for the Gentiles. 1 Timothy 2:7, says Paul is ordained a preacher, and an apostle, and a teacher of the Gentiles. In 2 Timothy 1:11, the Bible says Paul is appointed a preacher, and an apostle, and a teacher of the Gentiles. In Acts 9:15, Christ calls Paul His chosen vessel to bear Christ's name before the Gentiles. In Ephesians 3:2, we are told that God gave Paul the dispensation of grace to give to the Gentiles. Paul is God's messenger for us today in this present dispensation of God's grace to the Gentiles(nations).

In Galatians 2:1-9, we read some very important details about the apostle Paul and his ministry. However, to get background information about what Paul says in Galatians chapter 2, we first need to read Acts chapter 15. In Acts chapter 15, we learn that some Jews came down from Judea to Antioch and went behind Paul's back and told the Gentiles that they needed to keep the law of Moses in order to be saved (Acts 15:1-5). This perverts the gospel of our salvation that Paul received directly from the Lord Jesus Christ (Galatians 1:1-12). In order to set things straight, Paul and Barnabas go up to Jerusalem to communicate with Peter, James, and John, and the other apostles. The purpose of this meeting was for Paul to inform Israel's apostles about the revelations he had received from the

Lord, which they knew nothing about. Now, let's read Galatians 2:1-9, and then I will comment on these extremely important verses.

Galatians 2:1–9 (KJV)

¹ Then fourteen years after I went up again to Jerusalem with Barnabas, and took Titus with me also.

² And I went up by revelation, and communicated unto them that gospel which I preach among the Gentiles, but privately to them which were of reputation, lest by any means I should run, or had run, in vain.

³ But neither Titus, who was with me, being a Greek, was compelled to be circumcised:

⁴ And that because of false brethren unawares brought in, who came in privily to spy out our liberty which we have in Christ Jesus, that they might bring us into bondage:

⁵ To whom we gave place by subjection, no, not for an hour; that the truth of the gospel might continue with you.

⁶ But of these who seemed to be somewhat, (whatsoever they were, it maketh no matter to me: God accepteth no man's person:) for they who seemed to be somewhat in conference added nothing to me:

⁷ But contrariwise, when they saw that the gospel of the uncircumcision was committed unto me, as the gospel of the circumcision was unto Peter;

⁸ (For he that wrought effectually in Peter to the apostleship of the circumcision, the same was mighty in me toward the Gentiles:)

⁹ And when James, Cephas, and John, who seemed to be pillars, perceived the grace that was given unto me, they gave to me and Barnabas the right hands of fellowship; that we should go unto the heathen, and they unto the circumcision.

The information we read in these verses is Paul's personal account of the meeting that took place in Acts chapter 15. In verse 2, the Bible says that Paul went to Jerusalem by "revelation." This means that it was God which sent Paul to Jerusalem for a specific reason. In verse 2, we also see the reason for which the Lord sent him. The Bible says he was sent to communicate "that gospel which I preach among the Gentiles." This makes it very plain and clear that Paul is preaching a gospel message that James, Peter, and John knew nothing about. In verse 6, Paul tells us that in this conference James, Peter, and John "added nothing to me." After saying this, the first two words of verse 7 are "But contrariwise." This means in this conference they added no new information to Paul, "But contrariwise," means Paul added new information to them. This is extremely important to grasp! We see a transition taking place, whereas God is now giving new information to and through Paul and his ministry. God is no longer directly revealing new information to Israel's apostles. This is something most of professing Christendom has ignored for the most part and is a major cause of doctrinal error among Christians. In verse 7, we receive more vitally important information. Modern English Bibles published after the King James Bible, are corrupt and ruin what verse 7 is telling us. In Galatians 2:7, Paul tells us about two separate gospel messages. He says "the gospel of the uncircumcision" was committed to him, and that "the gospel of the circumcision" was committed to Peter. We will speak in more detail about these two gospel messages shortly. In verse 9, we read that James, Cephas (Peter), and John would stay only with their ministry to the circumcision (believing Jews), and that Paul and Barnabas would go to the heathen (unsaved Jews and Gentiles). This agreement never changes.

3

The Gospel of Our Salvation

Three times in the Bible Paul says, "my gospel" (Romans 2:16) (Romans 16:25) (2 Timothy 2:8). This lets us know how exclusive and unique Paul's gospel message really is. The gospel that Paul preaches is the gospel of our salvation today in this present dispensation of grace to Gentiles. This gospel, which Paul calls "my gospel," was not a message he received from the other apostles. This message came to Paul directly from the Lord Jesus Christ (Galatians 1:11,12). In Romans 1:16, Paul declares his gospel of Christ to be "the power of God unto salvation to every one that believeth." In 1 Corinthians 15:1-4, Paul declares plainly what the gospel we trust alone to be saved is. The gospel we believe to receive eternal life (Romans 6:23) is "how that Christ died for our sins according to the scriptures; And that he was buried, and that he rose again the third day according to the scriptures." We see this message is according to the scriptures and not a mystery. What makes Paul's gospel a revealed mystery (Ephesians 6:19) is the fact that in this dispensation of grace (Ephesians 3:1-4) every person that believes this gospel alone to receive forgiveness of sins and the gift of eternal life, is instantly sealed with the holy Spirit unto the day of redemption (Ephesians 1:13) (Ephesians 4:30). The instant we believe this gospel; we are baptized by the Spirit of God into the body of Christ (1 Corinthians 12:13; 1 Corinthians 12:27). We are now identified NOT as a nation, but rather we are "the body of Christ" (1 Corinthians 12:27). We are now a "new creature" (2 Corinthians 5:17) (Galatians 6:15), which is called "one new man" (Ephesians 2:15).

We are now members of Christ's body, flesh, and bones (Ephesians 5:30), and Christ is our Head (Ephesians 1:22,23) (Colossians 1:18). We are instantly justified by faith (Romans 5:1), and we have received all spiritual blessings in heavenly places (Ephesians 1:3). We are now quickened together with Christ and seated in heavenly places in Christ (Ephesians 2:5-7). These things are what makes our gospel a revealed mystery kept secret since the world began (Romans 16:25). Another thing that makes our gospel a revealed mystery is the fact that Gentiles can preach it to other Gentiles, without Israel being involved in any way. According to God's prophetic program with Israel, they are to be a kingdom of priests between God and the Gentiles (Exodus 19:6) (Isaiah 61:6) (1 Peter 2:9). During this present mystery dispensation in which God is forming His new creature (the body of Christ), Israel has no special standing. Today, Jews or Gentiles which believe the gospel of our salvation are instantly baptized by the Spirit of God into the body of Christ (Galatians 3:26-28). Paul preaches the death, burial, and resurrection of Christ according to the revelation of the mystery kept secret since the world began (Romans 16:25) (Ephesians 3:1-12) (Colossians 1:25-27). What has just been laid out are details about what Galatians 2:7 calls the gospel of the uncircumcision. Next, we will look at details about what Galatians 2:7 calls the gospel of the circumcision, which was committed unto Peter.

4

Israel's Gospel

Now that we have detailed the gospel of Christ, which Paul three times calls "my gospel," we will now detail Peter's gospel of the circumcision. When the Bible speaks about the "circumcision" it is talking about Jews and the nation of Israel (Ephesians 2:11). God raised up Abraham to bring forth His chosen nation Israel in Genesis chapter 12. In Genesis 17:10-14, God makes the covenant of circumcision between Himself and Abraham and Abraham's seed in the flesh, which is Israel. The gospel of the circumcision is a progressive revelation, which begins with Abraham in Genesis 12:1-7. This gospel message begins with God promising that out of Abraham would come forth a great nation, and that He would give Abraham and his seed (Israel) a land they would possess forever (Genesis 17:8). As we move through the Old Testament, God reveals that through the seed of David, that God Himself would sit on the throne as Israel's King (Psalm 132:11) (Isaiah 43:15). When we move into Matthew, Mark, Luke, and John, we see that God was manifest in the flesh through the seed of David (1 Timothy 3:16) (2 Timothy 2:8), which is Jesus Christ, the Son of God. The gospel message in these four books is called the gospel of the kingdom (Matthew 4:23) (Mark 1:14). The message to Israel at that time was "repent ye, and believe the gospel." The word "repent" in the Bible simply means to have a change of mind from the heart. The Jews needed to acknowledge they were sinners and change their minds from unbelief to believing Jesus is the Son of God (the Christ). They also need to prove their faith by getting water baptized to receive remission of sins. Jesus Christ is the King and His presence in Israel meant their promised kingdom was at hand. However, the majority of Israel rejected the King in unbelief and crucified Him. Once the Lord Jesus had called out a believing remnant, while the rest of Israel stumbled in unbelief, the kingdom was no longer "at hand" (Matthew 23:37,38) (Acts 1:6,7).

Israel's gospel of the circumcision (Galatians 2:7), which was also called the gospel of the kingdom in Matthew, Mark, Luke, and John, was about believing Jesus is the Christ (the Son of God), and it did not include Christ's death, burial, and resurrection. We looked at this already, however it is so important, we will look at it again. In Luke 9:6, it says the apostles were going everywhere preaching the gospel. When we move forward to Luke 18:31-34, we see very clearly that the apostles knew nothing about the Lord's death, burial, and resurrection. In John 20:4-9, we see that even after the Lord rose from the dead, that Peter and John as it says in John 20:9, "knew not the scripture, that he must rise from the dead." In Matthew, Mark, Luke, and John, when it speaks about believing in Jesus, it simply means believing Jesus is the Son of God that will be the King of the kingdom. This is why the Bible calls it the gospel of the kingdom. This is the gospel of God for Israel. Israel's gospel is a progressive message that began with the promise made to Abraham, concerning a great nation and a land. Afterwards, God adds to this message with the promise made to David about a King and kingdom. When we move into the book of Acts, Peter and the rest of Israel's apostles are still preaching the gospel of the kingdom. However, a further revelation about Christ's resurrection is added to the message. In Mark 16:16, the Lord said to Peter and the others, that "He that believeth and is baptized shall be saved." Somewhere around ten days after this, on the day of Pentecost, in Acts 2:36-38, Peter tells the Jews to "Repent, and be baptized every one of you in the name of Jesus Christ for the remission of sins, and ye shall receive the gift of the Holy Ghost." The word "repent" in the Bible simply means to have a change of mind from the heart. In Mark 16:16, the Lord says believe and be baptized to be saved, and in Acts 2:38, Peter says repent and be baptized. So, when Peter tells the Jews to repent, he simply means they need to change their minds from unbelief to believing Jesus is the Son of God and that He has been raised from the dead. Also, Peter makes it clear that when Christ returns, He will set up the promised kingdom (Acts 3:18-21). This is what the gospel of the circumcision is, which Paul says in Galatians 2:7, was committed unto Peter. This is the gospel of God for Israel.

5

The Hebrew Epistles

We will now look at what can rightly be called the Hebrew epistles. The Hebrew epistles are the books of Hebrews through Revelation. These books are written to and about the believing remnant of Israel. The main focus of the remnant's faith is that Jesus is the Christ, the Son of God (1 John 5:1) (1John 5:5). In John 11:24-27, Jesus asks Martha what she believes, and in verse 27, she says "I believe that thou art the Christ, the Son of God, which should come into the world." When we move into the Hebrew epistles, we see they have an understanding of Christ's Blood atonement for our sins. However, the focus of their faith is trusting Jesus is the Son of God, just like it is in Matthew, Mark, Luke, and John. In 1 John 5:1, it says "Whosoever believeth that Jesus is the Christ is born of God." In 1 John 5:5, it says "Who is he that overcometh the world, but he that believeth Jesus is the Son of God?" In 1 Thessalonians 4:14, Paul gives the qualification for those who will meet the Lord in the air, and he says, "For if we believe that Jesus died and rose again." We in the body of Christ believe Jesus is the Son of God, but the focus of our faith is on the Son of God's death, burial, and resurrection. The believing remnant of Israel believe Jesus died and rose again, but their faith is focused on who He is as the promised Messiah (Christ) from the Old Testament. We are currently under the mystery dispensation of God's grace to Gentiles. However, before this was revealed to Paul, Christ came to bring grace to Israel (John 1:17) by accomplishing everything necessary for God's new covenant with Israel (Hebrews 8:7-13). The old covenant was the law of Moses, in which Israel needed to have faith in God and perform according to what the law required. In the new covenant (Jeremiah 31:31-34), God will give believing Israel the Spirit of grace (Hebrews 10:29) and cause them to have the works that the covenant requires (Ezekiel 36:24-28). Israel is in a covenant relationship with God. This means to receive God's blessings, they need to do the works that the covenant requires. Israel broke the old covenant because our sinful flesh cannot perfectly keep God's laws. The new covenant is a covenant of grace because God will divinely enable believing Israel to keep the covenant (Hebrews 8:7-13). They will not be fully under the new covenant until they go through the "great tribulation" (Matthew 24:21), and Christ returns to wipe out His enemies and set up the thousand-year kingdom on earth (Revelation chapters 19 and 20).

Today as members of the body of Christ, in this present dispensation of God's grace to Gentiles, we receive eternal life and eternal security (once saved always saved) the moment we believe the gospel of our salvation (Ephesians 1:13; Ephesians 4:30). We are not in a covenant with God, rather we have a simple and clear grace through faith salvation (Ephesians 2:8,9). Israel is in a covenant relationship with God. A covenant is an agreement between two or more parties. This means that in order for Israel to receive their blessings and salvation from God, they need to fulfill the terms of their covenant with God. In the Hebrew epistles, Israel is in a transition from the old covenant (law of Moses) to the new covenant of grace (Hebrews 8:13). Under the new covenant, God by His Spirit, divinely enables them to perform the works of the covenant (1 John 3:24). In Matthew, Mark, Luke, and John, as well as Hebrews through Revelation, Israel's salvation depends on their faith plus works (James 2:24; Revelation 2:26). In Matthew 6:14,15, they must forgive others, or God will not forgive them. In John 15:10–14, they are the Lord's friends only if they keep His commandments. In Hebrews 3:14, they are made partakers of Christ only if they continue in the faith until they die or until the Lord returns. In Hebrews 6:4-6, if they fall away from the faith they lose salvation. In Hebrews 6:7, it explains that the believer which produces the fruit of good works gets blessed, then verse 8 explains the person which does not have the fruit of good works will be burned. In James 2:24, a person must have faith and works to be justified. In 1 John 2:4, the person that does not keep the commandments is lost.

In Acts 2:38, Peter tells Israel that if they repent (change their minds from unbelief to believing Jesus is the resurrected Son of God) and get water baptized, they will receive the gift of the Holy Ghost. During the time of Israel's transition from the old to the new covenant, once they receive the Holy Ghost, they have salvation, as long as they continue in the faith. Hebrews 6:4,5 says, after they are made partakers of the Holy Ghost, they get a taste of the powers of the world to come. They do not get the full powers of the new covenant, but a taste. This is speaking about God working in them to produce the required works (Hebrews 13:21). The only real condition for their salvation is that they continue in the faith, because if they do, God's Spirit causes them to produce the good works. However, Hebrews 6:4-6 and Hebrews 10:26-29, declare that if they wilfully sin and fall away from the faith in Christ, they lose salvation, and it is impossible to renew them again unto repentance. This means that if they quit believing they will go to hell. As long as they continue in the faith, the Holy Ghost will perform in them as the "Spirit of grace" (Hebrews 10:29) and divinely enable them to produce the good works their covenant requires (Hebrews 13:20,21). So, once they believe and get water baptized, they receive the gift of the Holy Ghost. However, if they fall away from the faith, they lose eternal life. The Holy Ghost is their "gift" (Acts 2:38) that enables them to perform according to their covenant. Today in the body of Christ, we have the Holy Ghost (1 Corinthians 6:19), but our "gift" is eternal life (Romans 6:23).

6

The Body of Christ

The body of Christ is a new creature (Galatians 6:15) that God is forming in this current mystery dispensation of His grace to Gentiles (Ephesians 3:1-9). In this present dispensation, the nation of Israel is fallen (Romans 11:11). Today the nation Israel has no special standing before God. They will be God's focus once again after the body of Christ is complete and caught up out of this world, in what is commonly called the rapture (1 Thessalonians 4:14-17). Today Israel is just a nation among the nations and Jews and Gentiles are in the same position. The gospel is available to everyone (Romans 1:16). The moment a person believes the gospel; they are baptized by the Spirit of God into the body of Christ (1 Corinthians 12:13). Saved people today are not a nation, but rather our identification is "the body of Christ, and members in particular" (1 Corinthians 12:27). The body of Christ is neither Jew nor Gentile, and neither male nor female (Galatians 3:28). The Bible calls the body of Christ a new creature (2 Corinthians 5:17), and one new man (Ephesians 2:15). Christ is the Head, and we are the body (Colossians 1:18). Today we are saved by grace through faith and our works have nothing to do with how we get saved (Romans 4:5) (Ephesians 2:8,9). However, after we get saved, the Bible tells us that we should increase in the knowledge of God (Colossians 1:10) and walk in good works (Ephesians 2:10). Though our works play no part in how we receive salvation, we will be judged according to our works at the "judgment seat of Christ" (Romans 14:10-12). At this Judgment each member of the body will receive rewards or loss of rewards based on our works (1 Corinthians 3:9-15). However, every member of the body of Christ receives all spiritual blessings in heavenly places, as well as a position in heavenly places (Ephesians 1:3) (Ephesians 2:4-7). We have a home not on the earth, but rather eternal in the heavens (2 Corinthians 5:1). We will be in a position to judge angels (1 Corinthians 6:3). We will receive eternal bodies fashioned like unto Jesus Christ's glorious body (Philippians 3:20,21). God has family in heaven and earth (Ephesians 3:14,15). The body of Christ will be in the heavens and Israel will be on the earth. We will detail this later in this book. The Bible tells us multiple times that Paul was given information about a mystery that God had kept secret since the world began (Romans 16:25) (Ephesians 3:1-12) (Colossians 1:25-27). The main focus of the mystery is God's "new creature" the body of Christ, and our position in God's eternal will. The information and doctrines concerning the body of Christ are found NOWHERE outside of Paul's books of Romans through Philemon. The mystery concerning the body of Christ is only revealed in these 13 books. In the book of Romans, chapters 9,10, and 11, tell us information about Israel's past, present, and future. The context and focus of these three chapters are about Israel (Romans 9:1-5) (Romans 10:1) (Romans 11:1,2). This is something that is important to understand because thinking Romans 10:9-13 is Paul telling us the gospel of our salvation is a very common error and has caused a lot of confusion among Bible students. Paul declares our gospel and things concerning salvation for the body of Christ in Romans chapters 1 through 8. In Romans chapter 11 the Gentiles graffed into the tree became part of the nation Israel, such as Cornelius, his kinsmen, and near friends (Acts 10:24). This was made available to Gentiles starting in Acts chapter 10 and put on hold in Acts chapter 15 with Peter and Paul's agreement, declared in Galatians 2:9. The opportunity for Gentiles to be graffed into Israel will be available again after this present dispensation of grace ends. A whole book could and should be written to explain Romans chapters 9 through 11.

7

The Body of Christ and Israel

The first verse in the Bible says that God created the heaven and the earth. This verse tells us that God has a purpose for heaven and earth. In Ephesians 3:15, the Bible tells us that God has family in heaven and earth. We in the body of Christ and the believing remnant of Israel are both citizens of the household of God. Both the body of Christ and believing Israel are the family of God. However, God will fulfill His purpose in the heavens through the body of Christ and He will fulfill His purpose on earth through the holy nation and royal priesthood, which is Israel.

All the promises and prophecy concerning the nation of Israel pertain to the earth. In Psalms 37:9, the Bible says that Israel shall inherit the earth. Psalm 37:29 tells us Israel will inherit land and dwell therein forever. In Matthew 5:5, the Lord Jesus Christ tells Israel they will inherit the earth. God has prepared a literal kingdom that will come down from heaven to earth in which Israel will rule the earth as kings and priests forever. Matthew 6:10 says, "Thy kingdom come. Thy will be done in earth, as it is in heaven." In Deuteronomy 11:21, the Bible says, "in the land which the LORD sware unto your fathers to give them, as the days of heaven upon the earth." In the books of Matthew, Mark, Luke, and John, when it speaks of the kingdom, the kingdom of heaven, or the kingdom of God, the Bible is talking about Israel's kingdom on earth. In Matthew 19:27,28, we learn that when Christ sets up the kingdom on earth, that Israel's twelve apostles will judge the twelve tribes of Israel. In Revelation 2:26, we learn that the believing remnant of Israel will have power over the nations on earth. In Revelation 5:10, the Bible tells us that those which overcome the antichrist in the great tribulation will be kings and priests, and "shall reign on the earth." Jeremiah 7:7 says, Israel will dwell in the land for ever and ever.

The Bible tells us that the promises, blessings, and dominion concerning the body of Christ are not on earth, but rather in heavenly places. Just as God will fulfill His eternal purpose for the earth through the nation Israel, He will fulfill His eternal purpose for the heavens through His new creature, the church, which is the body of Christ. In Ephesians 1:3, the Bible tells us we have been blessed with all spiritual blessings in heavenly places. In Ephesians 2:4-7, we learn that we have been quickened together with Christ. This is very unique and speaks to the fact that we have instant eternal security, when we believe the gospel. In Ephesians 1:13 and 4:30, we learn that the moment we believe the gospel, we are sealed with the holy Spirit unto the day of redemption. These verses make it clear we have eternal security or once saved always saved, in this present dispensation of God's grace. This is a doctrine that is unique for us in the body of Christ. The believing remnant of Israel must endure to the end of their life or until Christ returns, without falling away from the faith, if they fall away, they lose eternal life and cannot repent and get saved again (Matthew 24:13) (Hebrews 3:14) (Hebrews 6:4-6) (Hebrews 10:26-29). Also, in Ephesians 2:4-7, the Bible tells the body of Christ that we have a position in Christ, in heavenly places. In Colossians 3:2, the Bible tells us "Set your affection on things above, not on things on the earth." This is completely opposite than Israel, which has the hope of an eternal kingdom on earth. In 2 Corinthians 5:1, the Bible tells the body of Christ, that we have a home which is eternal in the heavens. In 1 Corinthians 6:3, we are told that we shall judge angels. Remember that Peter, James, John, and believing Israel are told they will rule over nations on earth (Matthew 19:27,28) (Revelation 2:26,27) (Revelation 5:10). We in the body of Christ are members of God's new creature that He is forming to operate in the heavenly places. We only learn about the body of Christ in the thirteen books of Romans through Philemon. Outside of these thirteen books there is no information about the body of Christ. We can glean some things from the book of Acts, but the focus of the book of Acts is Israel. This book does reveal Paul taking the gospel of grace to the Gentile world, but the focus is how Israel in the majority rejected Peter and his message, as well as Paul and his message.

In Chronicles 29:11, we learn that the kingdom of God includes all that is in heaven and earth. As members of the body of Christ, we are told in Colossians 1:13, that we are already translated into God's kingdom. We receive an instant and present standing in the kingdom of God. In 2 Peter 1:10,11, Peter tells the believing remnant of Israel that their entrance into the kingdom is something in their future, if they do not fall. They must endure in the faith until the end of their life or until the Lord returns at the end of the great tribulation, to set up the kingdom on earth. The whole kingdom of God includes the heavenly places, where the body of Christ will judge angels, and the earth, where Israel will judge nations.

There are different baptisms in the Bible. In Matthew 3:11, we see three different baptisms in one verse. This verse tells us there is a baptism with water, with the Holy Ghost, and with fire. In Hebrews 6:2, the Bible talks about "the doctrine of baptisms" (plural). The word "baptism" can only be defined by studying how it is used in the Bible's context. Many fight and argue about this word, because they want to make it fit the tradition of their particular denomination. Dictionaries are not helpful, because the word is a transliteration from the Greek. Dictionary definitions are biased and not very helpful because different dictionaries give different definitions. I will give you my definition based on studying the word in the Bible. Baptism simply means to be joined together for identification. In John 3:22-25, the Bible calls baptism a "purifying." Water baptism is something that specifically pertains to Israel and their priesthood. Israel will be a kingdom of priests on the earth (Exodus 19:6) (Isaiah 61:6) (1 Peter 2:9). In Numbers 8:6,7, the Levites, which were the priests under the law of Moses, are required to receive a water "purifying" in order to be fit for the priesthood. This was a water baptism. In the books of Matthew, Mark, Luke, John, and Acts, the Lord is calling out a believing remnant from Israel. Israel's remnant will be a kingdom of priests, and priests need to receive a water baptism to be fit for the priesthood. This is why water baptism is required under Israel's gospel of the kingdom. The Lord Jesus Christ in Matthew, Mark, Luke, and John, was preparing to be Israel's High Priest (Hebrews 3:1), this is why He needed to receive water baptism from John the Baptist (Matthew 3:13-17).

In the body of Christ, we are a new creature. We are not members of a nation or priesthood, but rather Ephesians 5:30 tells us "For we are members of his body, of his flesh, and of his bones." We must always keep in mind that in this present dispensation of God's grace to Gentiles, we follow the apostle Paul's pattern as our example of how to follow, serve, and worship Jesus Christ. In 1 Timothy 1:16, the Bible tells us Paul is the pattern for us today. In 1 Corinthians 11:1, the Bible tells us to follow Paul as he follows Christ. Paul did water baptize some people in the book of Acts. However, in Acts 26:16, we see Paul did not receive all the revelations for the body of Christ at one time, but rather he was receiving progressive revelations. By the time Paul wrote 1 Corinthians, the Lord told Paul not to baptize but preach the gospel. In 1 Corinthians 1:17, Paul says "For Christ sent me not to baptize, but to preach the gospel." After making this important statement, Paul in the same epistle says in 1 Corinthians 4:16, that we are to follow him. In this same epistle (1 Corinthians 11:1) he tells us to follow him as he follows Christ. Remember, Paul is our pattern for how we are to serve Christ. So, if Christ sent Paul not to baptize, but to preach the gospel, then you and I are also sent not to baptize, but to preach the gospel. In Ephesians 4:5, the Bible tells us in this present dispensation there is one baptism. In 1 Corinthians 12:13, the Bible tells us the Spirit of God baptizes us into the body of Christ. This is the one baptism for us today, and there is no water involved. This is a spiritual baptism we receive when we believe the gospel. In Colossians 2:11-13, the Bible tells us this baptism is made without men's hands, and that it is the operation of God. In Romans 6:3,4, Galatians 3:27, and Colossians 2:11-13, the Bible is talking about the Spirit of God baptizing us into Christ's death, burial, and resurrection. The Spirit of God performs this baptism and no water is involved. Water baptism is not for our participation today, and it only causes division among Christians. The denominations that teach a person needs to be water baptized to be saved, pervert the gospel of our salvation. If a person is trusting in water baptism to be saved, and not Christ alone, they are believing in vain. Those that believe in vain are not saved, and on their way to hell (1 Corinthians 15:1-4). Believing in vain means a person believes for no purpose. We trust Christ and believe the gospel for the purpose of receiving forgiveness of sins and the gift of eternal life. Any person who says they believe the gospel and at the same time believe they need to be water baptized, keep sacraments, or perform good works to be saved, is believing in vain. We are saved by grace through faith, not of works (Ephesians 2:8,9).

The word "church" in the Bible simply means a called out assembly. The word church can refer to the believing remnant of Israel (Acts 2:47). The word church can refer to Jews that followed Moses (Acts 7:38). The word church can refer to the one body of Christ (Ephesians 1:22,23). The word church can refer to a local assembly (1 Corinthians 16:19). When we see the word church, the scripture's context will identify which called-out assembly is being talked about. In 1 Corinthians 1:2, Paul says "unto the church of God which is at Corinth," meaning an assembly of local believers. In Galatians 1:13, Paul speaks about when he persecuted the "church of God," meaning the believing remnant of Israel. In 2 Thessalonians 1:4, Paul says "the churches of God," meaning local assemblies of saved people. All of this is to show that the Bible uses the word church in various ways. Ephesians 4:4 tells us there is one body. This is the new creature, the body of Christ. In Colossians 1:18, the one body which Christ is the Head of, is called the church. The believing remnant of Israel is a church of God. The body of Christ is a church of God. When we meet with a group of believers, this too, is a church of God. When anyone anywhere on the planet believes the gospel of our salvation, they instantly become a member of the one body of Christ, which is the church all saved people in this dispensation belong to. Rightly dividing the word of truth means rightly dividing Israel and the body of Christ. Many speak about the difference between Israel and the church. That is not specific enough, because Israel is also called a church.

8

Conclusion

The first word in the book of Genesis to the last word of Revelation are God's inspired and preserved words. The King James Bible is God's perfect and pure words in English. The most important thing for any person is that they believe the gospel and receive the gift of eternal life. The next most important thing is to become a Bible believer. This means we take the words of the Bible we hold in our hand as the highest authority in this world. In 1 Thessalonians 2:13, the Bible says the word of God works effectually in us, when we believe it. When we read the Bible every day and believe it, those pure words take effect in our hearts and change our lives. God's words changed my life. If you would like to read a clear and concise book about the Bible version issue, I strongly recommend a little book I have written titled "Pure Words."

After we get saved and become Bible believers, the next most important thing is to obey 2 Timothy 2:15. This verse says, "Study to shew thyself approved unto God, a workman that needeth not to be ashamed, rightly dividing the word of truth." The purpose of this book has been to teach you how to rightly divide the word of truth. There are two major programs in God's word. The first program is that which Peter declares in Acts 3:21 "which God hath spoken by the mouth of all his holy prophets since the world began." This is God's prophetic program and pertains to Israel and the earth. The second major program in God's word is what Paul says in Romans 16:25 "according to the revelation of the mystery, which was kept secret since the world began." This is God's mystery program and pertains to the body of Christ and the heavens. The information about the body of Christ and God's mystery program is found only in Paul's epistles of Romans through Philemon. All the Bible is profitable, and we need to study all of it. However, we must rightly divide God's prophetic program from His mystery program.

(Ephesians 3:9) 9 And to make all men see what is the fellowship of the mystery, which from the beginning of the world hath been hid in God, who created all things by Jesus Christ:

Also from Jeffery Drake, Jr.

Pure Words:
Identifying the King James Bible as God's Pure Words in English

In *Pure Words*, Jeffery Drake, Jr. presents a clear and compelling defense of the King James Bible as the preserved words of God in English. Written with conviction and humility, the book walks readers through the history of the biblical text, the difference between the Received and Critical Greek texts, and God's promise of preservation found in Scripture itself.

Drake traces the line of faithful transmission from the apostles through the Reformation era to the publication of the King James Bible in 1611, exposing the errors of modern textual criticism and affirming that God's pure words remain available today. Combining sound reasoning, scriptural proof, and personal testimony, *Pure Words* strengthens the believer's confidence in the Bible as the final authority in all matters of faith and doctrine.

Available from Trust House Publishers

www.TrustHousePublishers.com

www.ingramcontent.com/pod-product-compliance
Lightning Source LLC
Chambersburg PA
CBHW061721120626
46550CB00003B/1321